THE
GAY
AGENDA

UNIVERSE

Published by UNIVERSE PUBLISHING
A Division of Rizzoli International Publications, Inc.
300 Park Avenue South
New York, NY 10010
www.rizzoliusa.com

© 2019 Universe Publishing
All rights reserved.

Design by Celina Carvalho
Printed in Hong Kong, PRC

If you fall in love with a boy, you fall in love with a boy. The fact that many Americans consider it a disease says more about them than it does about homosexuality.

JAMES BALDWIN

.... , 20 ....

.... Monday

.... Tuesday

.... Wednesday

.... Thursday

.... Friday

.... Saturday

.... Sunday

I learned compassion from being discriminated against. Everything bad that's ever happened to me has taught me compassion.

ELLEN DEGENERES

I think being gay is a blessing,
and it's something I am thankful
for every single day.

ANDERSON COOPER

.... , 20 ....

.... Monday

.... Tuesday

.... Wednesday

.... Thursday

.... Friday

.... Saturday

.... Sunday

...., 20 ....

.... Monday

.... Tuesday

.... Wednesday

.... Thursday

.... Friday

.... Saturday

.... Sunday

Never be bullied into silence.
Never allow yourself to be made
a victim. Accept no one's definition
of your life; define yourself.

HARVEY FIERSTEIN

What is straight?
A line can be straight, or a street,
but the human heart,
oh, no, it's curved like a road
through mountains.

TENNESSEE WILLIAMS

.... , 20 ....

.... Monday

.... Tuesday

.... Wednesday

.... Thursday

.... Friday

.... Saturday

.... Sunday

.... , 20 ....

.... Monday

.... Tuesday

.... Wednesday

.... Thursday

.... Friday

.... Saturday

.... Sunday

Every gay and lesbian person who has been lucky enough to survive the turmoil of growing up is a survivor. Survivors always have an obligation to those who will face the same challenges.

BOB PARIS

I've been embraced by a new community. That's what happens when you're finally honest about who you are; you find others like you.

CHAZ BONO

.... , 20 ....

.... Monday

.... Tuesday

.... Wednesday

.... Thursday

.... Friday

.... Saturday

.... Sunday

.... , 20 ....

.... Monday

.... Tuesday

.... Wednesday

.... Thursday

.... Friday

.... Saturday

.... Sunday

If a bullet should enter my brain, let that bullet destroy every closet door.

HARVEY MILK

It is revolutionary for any
trans person to choose to be
seen and visible in a world that
tells us we should not exist.

LAVERNE COX

.... , 20 ....

.... Monday

.... Tuesday

.... Wednesday

.... Thursday

.... Friday

.... Saturday

.... Sunday

.... , 20 ....

.... Monday

.... Tuesday

.... Wednesday

.... Thursday

.... Friday

.... Saturday

.... Sunday

Personally, coming out was one of the most important things I've ever done, lifting from my shoulders the millstone of lies that I hadn't even realized I was carrying.

SIR IAN MCKELLEN

Equality means more than passing laws. The struggle is really won in the hearts and minds of the community, where it really counts.

BARBARA GITTINGS

.... , 20 ....

.... Monday

.... Tuesday

.... Wednesday

.... Thursday

.... Friday

.... Saturday

.... Sunday

.... , 20 ....

.... Monday

.... Tuesday

.... Wednesday

.... Thursday

.... Friday

.... Saturday

.... Sunday

They say that this country is free, and they say that this country is equal, but it is not equal if it's sometimes.

LADY GAGA

So let me be clear: I'm proud to be gay, and I consider being gay among the greatest gifts God has given me.

TIM COOK

.... , 20 ....

.... Monday

.... Tuesday

.... Wednesday

.... Thursday

.... Friday

.... Saturday

.... Sunday

...., 20.............

.... Monday

.... Tuesday

.... Wednesday

.... Thursday

.... Friday

.... Saturday

.... Sunday

We should indeed keep calm in the face of difference, and live our lives in a state of inclusion and wonder at the diversity of humanity.

GEORGE TAKEI

I am young, yes, but what I have learned is that love–the beauty of it, the joy of it, and yes, even the pain of it–is the most incredible gift to give and to receive as a human being. And we deserve to experience love fully, equally, without shame, and without compromise.

ELLEN PAGE

.... , 20 ....

.... Monday

.... Tuesday

.... Wednesday

.... Thursday

.... Friday

.... Saturday

.... Sunday

.... , 20 ....

.... Monday

.... Tuesday

.... Wednesday

.... Thursday

.... Friday

.... Saturday

.... Sunday

I am a strong, black, lesbian woman.
Every single time I say it,
I feel so much better.

BRITTNEY GRINER

When an individual is protesting society's refusal to acknowledge his dignity as a human being, his very act of protest confers dignity on him.

BAYARD RUSTIN

.... , 20 ....

.... Monday

.... Tuesday

.... Wednesday

.... Thursday

.... Friday

.... Saturday

.... Sunday

.... , 20 ....

.... Monday

.... Tuesday

.... Wednesday

.... Thursday

.... Friday

.... Saturday

.... Sunday

To live is the rarest thing in the world. Most people exist, that is all.

OSCAR WILDE

I believe that telling our stories, first to ourselves and then to one another and the world, is a revolutionary act.

JANET MOCK

.... , 20 ....

.... Monday

.... Tuesday

.... Wednesday

.... Thursday

.... Friday

.... Saturday

.... Sunday

.... , 20 ....

.... Monday

.... Tuesday

.... Wednesday

.... Thursday

.... Friday

.... Saturday

.... Sunday

We needed something to express
our joy, our beauty, our power.
And the rainbow did that.

GILBERT BAKER

No government has the right
to tell its citizens when or whom
to love. The only queer people are
those who don't love anybody.

RITA MAE BROWN

.... , 20 ....

.... Monday

.... Tuesday

.... Wednesday

.... Thursday

.... Friday

.... Saturday

.... Sunday

.... , 20 ....

.... Monday

.... Tuesday

.... Wednesday

.... Thursday

.... Friday

.... Saturday

.... Sunday

The beauty of standing up
for your rights is others see you
standing and stand up as well.

CASSANDRA DUFFY

The single best thing about coming out of the closet is that nobody can insult you by telling you what you've just told them.

RACHEL MADDOW

.... , 20 ....

.... Monday

.... Tuesday

.... Wednesday

.... Thursday

.... Friday

.... Saturday

.... Sunday

.... , 20 ....

.... Monday

.... Tuesday

.... Wednesday

.... Thursday

.... Friday

.... Saturday

.... Sunday

You look ridiculous if you dance
You look ridiculous if you don't dance
So you might as well
dance.

GERTRUDE STEIN

When I talk to young people,
I always tell them the biggest lesson
I learned was that you shouldn't
care about the outcome. If it fails,
it fails. Every failure will groom you
for your next big reward.

RYAN MURPHY

.... , 20 ....

.... Monday

.... Tuesday

.... Wednesday

.... Thursday

.... Friday

.... Saturday

.... Sunday

.... , 20 ....

.... Monday

.... Tuesday

.... Wednesday

.... Thursday

.... Friday

.... Saturday

.... Sunday

Being gay is a natural, normal,
beautiful variation on being human.
Period.

LARRY KRAMER

My LGBQTIA family, I see each and every one of you. The things that make us different, those are our superpowers. Every day when you walk out the door, put on your imaginary cape and go out there and conquer the world. Because the world would not be as beautiful as it is if we weren't in it.

LENA WAITHE

.... , 20 ....

.... Monday

.... Tuesday

.... Wednesday

.... Thursday

.... Friday

.... Saturday

.... Sunday

.... , 20 ....

.... Monday

.... Tuesday

.... Wednesday

.... Thursday

.... Friday

.... Saturday

.... Sunday

Fight for your lives before
it's someone else's job.

EMMA GONZALEZ

Hell hath no fury like
a drag queen scorned.

SYLVIA RIVERA

.... , 20 ....

.... Monday

.... Tuesday

.... Wednesday

.... Thursday

.... Friday

.... Saturday

.... Sunday

.... , 20 ....

.... Monday

.... Tuesday

.... Wednesday

.... Thursday

.... Friday

.... Saturday

.... Sunday

The right to life, liberty, and the pursuit of happiness means that each of us is free to go our own way, even if the ways some of us may choose to go seem sinful or shocking to our fellow citizens.

DAN SAVAGE

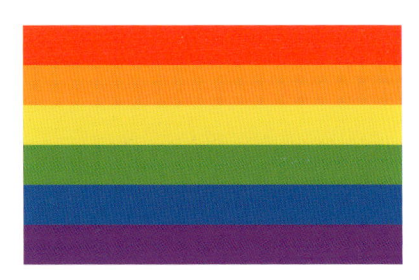

I was recently asked in an interview what it's like to be a gay athlete in sports. I said that it's exactly like being a straight athlete. Lots of hard work but usually done with better eyebrows.

ADAM RIPPON

.... , 20 ....

.... Monday

.... Tuesday

.... Wednesday

.... Thursday

.... Friday

.... Saturday

.... Sunday

.... , 20 ....

.... Monday

.... Tuesday

.... Wednesday

.... Thursday

.... Friday

.... Saturday

.... Sunday

At the end of the day,
we can endure much more
than we think we can.

FRIDA KAHLO

I have learned not to worry about love; but to honor its coming with all my heart.

ALICE WALKER

.... , 20 ....

.... Monday

.... Tuesday

.... Wednesday

.... Thursday

.... Friday

.... Saturday

.... Sunday

.... , 20 ....

.... Monday

.... Tuesday

.... Wednesday

.... Thursday

.... Friday

.... Saturday

.... Sunday

When you've seen prejudice, you understand that we aren't finished, that we're still perfecting this American experiment.

ANTHONY ROMERO

If your love for me requires that I hide parts of who I am, then you don't love me. Love is never a request for silence.

DERAY MCKESSON

.... , 20 ....

.... Monday

.... Tuesday

.... Wednesday

.... Thursday

.... Friday

.... Saturday

.... Sunday

.... , 20 ....

.... Monday

.... Tuesday

.... Wednesday

.... Thursday

.... Friday

.... Saturday

.... Sunday

I am transgender and this doesn't mean that I am unlovable.

LANA WACHOWSKI

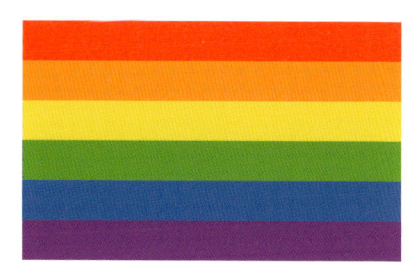

You can walk through life believing
in the goodness of the world,
or walk through life afraid of anyone
who thinks different than you and
trying to convert them to your
way of thinking.

ROSIE O'DONNELL

.... , 20 ....

.... Monday

.... Tuesday

.... Wednesday

.... Thursday

.... Friday

.... Saturday

.... Sunday

.... , 20 ....

.... Monday

.... Tuesday

.... Wednesday

.... Thursday

.... Friday

.... Saturday

.... Sunday

There's nothing wrong with going to bed with somebody of your own sex. . . . I just think people should be very free with sex—they should draw the line at goats.

ELTON JOHN

We are powerful because
we have survived.

AUDRE LORDE

.... , 20 ....

.... Monday

.... Tuesday

.... Wednesday

.... Thursday

.... Friday

.... Saturday

.... Sunday

.... , 20 ....

.... Monday

.... Tuesday

.... Wednesday

.... Thursday

.... Friday

.... Saturday

.... Sunday

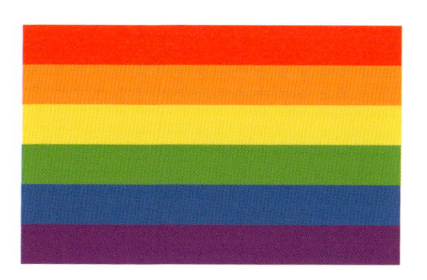

All of us who are openly gay are living and writing the history of our movement. We are no more–and no less–heroic than the suffragists and abolitionists of the nineteenth century; and the labor organizers, Freedom Riders, Stonewall demonstrators, and environmentalists of the twentieth century. We are ordinary people, living our lives, and trying, as civil-rights activist Dorothy Cotton said, to "fix what ain't right" in our society.

TAMMY BALDWIN

There's no right or wrong way to be gay. No right or wrong way to come out. It's your journey, do it the way you want to do it.

TAN FRANCE

.... , 20 ....

- Monday
- Tuesday
- Wednesday
- Thursday
- Friday
- Saturday
- Sunday

.... , 20 ....

.... Monday

.... Tuesday

.... Wednesday

.... Thursday

.... Friday

.... Saturday

.... Sunday

It's time to order your

THE
GAY
AGENDA

undated agenda

Take this form to your book or stationery dealer, or mail to:
UNIVERSE PUBLISHING
300 Park Avenue South
New York, NY 10010

Included is my check / money order for *The Gay Agenda*
(please make check payable to Universe Publishing):

_____ copies @ $15.99 each   _____

Postage/handling (Continental U.S. only): Add shipping zone rate   _____
(Zone rates: East $9.00; Midwest $10.00; West $11.00)
For shipping outside the Continental U.S., call 1-800-52-BOOKS for freight quote.

For multiple copies, add $1.00 per copy   _____

Subtotal   _____

New York State residents add 8.875% sales tax   _____
(on subtotal including shipping)

Total amount of check/money order enclosed   _____

Credit Card: ____ Amex ____ Disc ____ MC ____ Visa
Account Number _____
Exp. Date _____ Card Verification Code (3 or 4 digits) _____
Signature _____

Name _____
Address _____
City _____ State _____ Zip _____
Phone★ _____ Date _____
★Required for all credit card orders.

Please visit our website, www.rizzoliusa.com,
to download your copy of the illustrated calendar catalog.

.... , 20 ....

.... Monday

.... Tuesday

.... Wednesday

.... Thursday

.... Friday

.... Saturday

.... Sunday

.... , 20 ....

.... Monday

.... Tuesday

.... Wednesday

.... Thursday

.... Friday

.... Saturday

.... Sunday

My legacy would be that you don't have to give up anything. You can be chic but have a sense of humor, you can be sexy but comfortable, you can be timeless but fresh.

MICHAEL KORS

Everyone is both sexes in varying degrees. I am more of a woman than a man.

CHRISTINE JORGENSEN

.... , 20 ....

.... Monday

.... Tuesday

.... Wednesday

.... Thursday

.... Friday

.... Saturday

.... Sunday

.... , 20 ....

.... Monday

.... Tuesday

.... Wednesday

.... Thursday

.... Friday

.... Saturday

.... Sunday

Love is the big booming beat which covers up the noise of hate.

MARGARET CHO

We need to stop playing Privilege or Oppression Olympics because we'll never get anywhere until we find more effective ways of talking through difference. We should be able to say, "This is my truth," and have that truth stand without a hundred clamoring voices shouting, giving the impression that multiple truths cannot coexist.

ROXANE GAY

.... , 20 ....

.... Monday

.... Tuesday

.... Wednesday

.... Thursday

.... Friday

.... Saturday

.... Sunday

.... , 20 ....

.... Monday

.... Tuesday

.... Wednesday

.... Thursday

.... Friday

.... Saturday

.... Sunday

Just by being out you're doing your part. It's like recycling. You're doing your part for the environment if you recycle; you're doing your part for the gay movement if you're out.

MARTINA NAVRATILOVA

As minorities, we're on the fringe, and there's just something so wonderful about that perspective, something so inspiring. If you're part of that minority, you can make fun of those people while respecting them and lifting them up.

KATE MCKINNON

.... , 20 ....

.... Monday

.... Tuesday

.... Wednesday

.... Thursday

.... Friday

.... Saturday

.... Sunday

.... , 20 ....

.... Monday

.... Tuesday

.... Wednesday

.... Thursday

.... Friday

.... Saturday

.... Sunday

Don't postpone joy.

EDIE WINDSOR

If you can't love yourself,
how the hell are you gonna
love somebody else?

RUPAUL

.... , 20 ....

Monday

Tuesday

Wednesday

Thursday

Friday

Saturday

Sunday

.... , 20 ....

.... Monday

.... Tuesday

.... Wednesday

.... Thursday

.... Friday

.... Saturday

.... Sunday

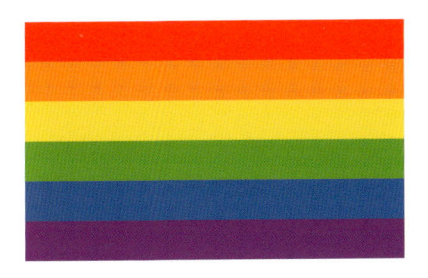

To be rendered powerless does not destroy your humanity. Your resilience is your humanity. The only people who lose their humanity are those who believe they have the right to render another human being powerless. They are the weak. To yield and not break, that is incredible strength.

HANNAH GADSBY

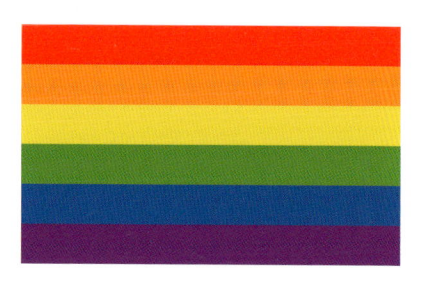

I don't want to be tolerated.
That offends my love of life
and of liberty.

JEAN COCTEAU

.... , 20 ....

.... Monday

.... Tuesday

.... Wednesday

.... Thursday

.... Friday

.... Saturday

.... Sunday

.... , 20 ....

.... Monday

.... Tuesday

.... Wednesday

.... Thursday

.... Friday

.... Saturday

.... Sunday

Openness may not completely disarm prejudice, but it's a good place to start.

JASON COLLINS

What do you mean you "don't believe in homosexuality"? It's not like the Easter Bunny, your belief isn't necessary.

LEA DELARIA

.... , 20 ....

.... Monday

.... Tuesday

.... Wednesday

.... Thursday

.... Friday

.... Saturday

.... Sunday